"Be Still and Know"

a journey through love in Japanese short form poetry

by

Svetlana Marisova
&
Ted van Zutphen

"Be still and know"

Copyright © 2012

Svetlana Marisova & Ted van Zutphen

Karakia Press
10/2011
karakiapress.com

ISBN 978-0-473-20664-2

*Edited, cover, design and cover
photographs by Ted van Zutphen*

haiga pictures and art:
'desert heat' - Saguaro Pictures
'desert thirst' - unnamed artist
'stretching' and 'blood sucker' - Dave Willis
'the spring dew' - family archives
'the weight' - Hannah van Zutphen-Kann
all other pictures by
Ted van Zutphen and Svetlana Marisova
Copyright to the owners.

Only connect! . . . Only connect the prose and the passion, and both will be exalted, and human love will be seen at its height. Live in fragments no longer. Only connect, and the beast and the monk, robbed of the isolation that is life to either, will die.

E. M. Forster ~ Howard's End

Introduction
by
Robert D. Wilson

The book you are about to read, Be Still and Know,
contains the haiku of Svetlana Marisova interspersed
with haiku written by her online soul-mate, Ted van
Zutphen, himself an excellent haiku poet. They met on
the Internet and began to share and write haiku
together forming an eternal bond. This book is not an
exchange of love-notes, nor a responsive stream of
consciousness. It's much stronger than this.
 Though close, the two never met each other in person,
but to them it felt as if they had. They come from
different backgrounds with different cultural
memories. Ted grew up in Holland, but lives in the
U.S and Svetlana, a Russian by birth, lived in New
Zealand from her early teens until her death.

summer dreams
the night thick with
datura

 Svetlana wrote this as she feared the return of an
earlier brain tumor. Cancer sometimes will take its
sweet time, coming, ebbing, coming again, and in
Marisova's case, it did return. She was hallucinating
on a summer night as if she had taken a dose of
datura, a poisonous weed used by some indigenous
tribes in religious rites to induce hallucinations. If
used wrong or given to the wrong person, they will
die an ugly death and suffer from hallucinations that
make the best horror movie look like Alice in
Wonderland.

Marisova was a fighter and refused to let the cancer and pain stop her from writing what I believe to be the finest haiku written since Issa. Fortunately, she didn't have to face the task of writing her poetry alone.

Ted van Zutphen, her on-line friend, was drawn into her world, and not by chance. Ted turned out to be an excellent haiku poet, one of the best.

He encouraged Marisova as she encouraged van Zutphen. The more they wrote, the closer they became, almost thinking what the other was thinking. The body of haiku produced from this symbiotic union is second to none, and I predict the poetry in this book will be remembered for centuries to come.

> *winter dawn —*
> *a doe's breath dissolves*
> *into the mist*

It hurt van Zutphen to see his soul-mate in such pain, and still insist on composing haiku, studying haiku, coupled with many hours of prayer and the study of God's Word. His haiku took on a voice he'd never used before and the result is symbiotic and totally in tune with Svetlana.

Poetry is a language few speak well or understand. It is a language prose cannot speak, a language spoken by the subconscious mind. Like zoka, nature's creative, unpredictable spirit, what is said can be unpredictable. The mind is complex and no two people think alike.

With haiku, a poet's subconscious mind joins together with the conscious mind and collectively enter the sacred halls of zoka. This is why haiku cannot be object- (mono, subjective) biased. The composition of a true haiku is the combination of three distinct parts (a poetic trinity) that defies explanation and Anglo-Western logic.

Instinctively Marisova and van Zutphen tapped into this realm. Marisova said I was her mentor, but I believe God was her mentor, and I was used to guide her in a small way. Ted's role was much greater. He believed in Marisova more than he believed in himself, encouraging her to continue when it would have been easier to give up and be with her maker. In essence, they grew whole as human beings through this short union; a wholeness they may never have found without the other. They both had an impish sense of humor, chatting online, by e-mail, messaging, whenever they could connect, laughing, crying, dreaming, feeding one another ideas, musing each other, building each other's self confidence on the way and helping each other to discover their poetic voice.

winter night . . .
in the hermitage
silent drums

red winds . . .
an angel's trumpet,
moon bathing

Svetlana Marisova

Ted van Zutphen

rose petals ---
the ceremony
of blood

the warmth
of your silence
winter heart

Svetlana Marisova and Ted van Zutphen are truly soul-mates. And I use 'are' on purpose rather than the expected 'were.' Through the magic of haiku and laughter they formed a bond, that created two outstanding poets, who affected the lives of many for the good and continue to do so via their words and spirits, to set a standard for other haiku poets to aspire to without being identical halves of a mush melon.

Foreword
by
Ted van Zutphen

This book is the culmination of a year and a half long
on-line relationship between Svetlana and me. It
started on the so-called "sarcasm pages" of facebook
and, through mischief and mayhem, ended up in the
world of English language Japanese short form poetry,
where it continues to this day even after the passing of
Svetlana on September 7th of 2011.

rua wai . . .	*two waters . . .*
na te kore te po	*from the void flows the night*
ki te whai-ao	*to the glimmer of dawn*

I am so happy I friended this marvelous young
woman, who led me into haiku as she was discovering
it herself. We grew up together through haiku and
after only a few short months the seed of this book
was born. It was only a year ago, that we agreed
October 2011 was our target date. Unfortunately
Svetlana never made it that far, but she did enjoy the
first chapter that I put together, before she was called
into His love.

As you read this book, keep in mind that there is no
chronology in most of our poetry exchange, I've merely
tried to weave the threads that ran through our
relationship, to create a timeless journey of the love we
experienced by being open to it, even worlds apart.

At the base of our haiku is our attempt to get deeper and further into the spirit that animates us, without getting all stuck up about it.

Svetlana:

".... spirit is the animating force in any creation - not a feeling, nothing seen, nothing heard, nothing smelt, nothing tasted, nothing touched. I think that this applies equally to haiku. Haiku embodies certain inherited Japanese aesthetic styles to catch the breath of the creator/poet. Within that, the individual haiku is limited only by the creative spirit harnessed by the writer. Anything becomes possible and we have barely begun to realise its potential."

Before losing her valiant fight with the tumour in her brain, she told me:

"I still want to write THAT haiku, but others keep flooding in… If I can, I want to notch my writing up another level, not to meet anyone's expectations, but to be authentic expressions of what is in me to say…

I am not likely going to achieve those heights of poetic power myself, but I can walk ahead and light the path for the ones who will… your style is unique and filled with organic energy; none can equal you in what you are doing… just do it, breathe it."

Personally, I think she did write THAT haiku and it's in this book … somewhere.

I designed and edited the book, based on some ideas Svetlana and I discussed and agreed on. Though connections between our poems run throughout the book, across pages and from page to page, little of it was written as any kind of linked verse,
In the first three chapters, you'll find Svetana's poems on the left (even) pages and mine on the right (odd), with un-noted exceptions in some sequences near the end of the third chapter. The fourth chapter is all her and the fifth is all my work. In the final chapter I have deviated from all identifying distinctions made previously, to let our story flow. By then I expect the reader will be thoroughly familiar with our different styles that it doesn't matter anyway. In any case, it's the poetry that matters... not the poet!

I hope you'll enjoy our journey through love.
Be Still and Know...

Finally, I want to thank Hansha Teki for his support and assistance in getting this labour of love to a finish, from helping me unearth some of her material to bringing the book online and to hardcopy as well.
Thanks also to Robert D. Wilson and Saša Važić for their belief in us, Dave Willis and my daughter Hannah for gracefully letting us use their art, our families and all our friends in real - and cyber life for their encouragement and love throughout these last two years, and we thank you, the reader, for being part of our journey.

"The personal life deeply lived always expands into truths beyond itself." ~ Svetlana

earthly thanks
we cannot forget . . .
distant star

kia kaha,
Ted

*This book is dedicated to
Svetlana's Mama, her Papa
and Natasha Nikonova,
the people who prepared her
to become the light she is.*

Seasons

(where our southern - and northern hemisphere meet, separate and connect)

winter calm . . .
the sound of light
liquefies

up stretched arms . . .
the winter cloud still
unknowing

double rainbow . . .
a monsoon cloud
fills the sun

full moon . . .
taranaki's hidden glow
awakens

incoming tide . . .
the writing fills
both sides

autumn dusk . . .
watching the tide
recede

new moon . . .
the light of
fresh snow

two haijin
on the same page . . .
new herring

snow drop—
the rite of spring . . .
tolls

harvest moon . . .
this quickening
of light

steam rises
from a cow pat —
autumn morning

singing alone
the child chains daisies ...
autumn dusk

spring brook . . .
your love chiming
in the breeze

spring fever —
even the bitch
curls her tail

narcissus —
Miles' trumpet cleaning
my winter blues . . .

morning frost —
the crackling sound
of our eyes

winter night . . .
the cat rubs herself
into a smile

winter chill —
still this outburst
of flowers

silent summer —
the sound of the guitar
still in his ears

summer heat —
between every dip
your cool smile

oh rose . . .
I do not want
to pluck you!

winter night . . .
in the hermitage
silent drums

snow blanket . . .
veiling the fire
within

for each feather
that blows in the wind —
a winter's tale

red winds . . .
an angel's trumpet,
moon bathing

summer heat . . .
the breeze carrying
a rumble

summer wind . . .
the old oak sheds
its bark

spring awakening —
the sound of water
in the mist

stillness —
even spring
is frozen

the old dog
learns a new trick —
spring planting

dawn moon . . .
the red river flows
into its past

night breath—
in, out, back and forth
of tree frogs

harvest—
even after dark
forbidden fruit

still pond —
shadow of a mayfly
in the depths

last breath
without knowing . . .
rising mist

end of spring . . .
immaculate in timing
if not conception

double moon . . .
the river flows
in between

floating
into the harbour . . .
haloed moon

autumn wind . . .
the different colours
of our memories

summer dreams . . .
the night thick with
datura

a young nun
resists the tides . . .
waxing moon

buttercup —
she picks the petals away
for an answer

blue eyes —
in the frozen pond
winter sky

snow drifts —
an angel spreads
her wings

mourning card —
he plucks a grey hair
from his eyebrow

rising sun —
the limb-loosening fire
in your eyes

rose petals —
the ceremony
of blood

honeysuckle —
the tremor of a smile
on tight lips

winter dawn —
a doe's breath dissolves
into the mist

the warmth
of your silence . . .
winter heart

a stream
below the ice . . .
spring whispers

<3

after dusk
I become your dream
silent conch

becoming one —
a man and a woman
and a blackbird

desert heat -
your arms embracing
my fire

Ted van Zutphen & Saguaro Pictures

rose hips —
how did I miss
the blooms?

what love is this
which finds you within me
filling the night?
you, who made this mystery,
rise with the sun in my heart

hidden spring . . .
all that cannot be expressed
spills over

frangipani —
even in my dreams,
that scent

shadows
of bare branches . . .
dreams,
painted in sun soaked snow
longing to awaken

mountain lake,
the spring sun
in its depths

goblet moon . . .
both of us cradling
an autumn night

valentine's day —
some mysteries remain
locked

this apple
the otherness of you
out of reach

winter dawn —
the crackling of ice
on the old pond

first date —
the rowboat
wobbles

prickly pear —
this blossom inviting
the sun

a stream trickles
beneath winter shadows…
sumi-e

flipping up,
flipping down . . . fish
out of water

maiden flower . . .
the deepening silence
of the veil

fertile valley . . .
the frozen waterfall
still flowing

a fish
catches the fishfly
catches a fish

spring mist —
behind the veil,
her tears

silent dance . . .
the distance between
pulsing in time

the dance
and the girl . . .
one

gentle breeze . . .
who sent me these
goosebumps

spring dance . . .
wrapping the universe
in our song

budding spring —
tomorrow's sunrise
now

summer shade . . .
a fallen fig
shows its flesh

zoo in spring . . .
behind the spectators
a tui sings

spring tension . . .
awakened hormones
winding up

winter lull . . .
dosed up for now on
dutch courage

a cardinal sings
in the key of love —
spring thaw

spring shower . . .
in the fountain
more rings

tulips —
the joy of spring
in december

night wildflowers —
a morepork calls
its own name

squelching mud
between her toes —
silent spring

Lake Baikal —
the hidden depths
of his eyes

a grackle,
ruffling its feathers . . .
and song

hot springs . . .
from your silent depths,
absorbing

blue eyes —
all they want to see,
all that's hidden

spring frenzy
the buck's ardour
dampens

new moon . . .
yearning for the light
that consumes her

reflected
in a tuatara's eye —
primeval light

a yearling
finds his stride . . .
second spring

ocean waves . . .
breaking in a language
i know

pole star —
in her eyes
hot chocolate

The Finding

suddenly I become small in your arms as you draw me to you melting me with such peace helplessly nestling into you and feeling the throb of your body glowing with tender desire for my melting to your touch and the ache that my softness passes into your blood

rippling pond
where his shadow falls . . .
fragrant breeze

the desire of your hands caressing the shape of my warming to you comes nearer and nearer to the very heart of me as I feel your tender flame melting me away fueling the rising torch pressing against me with an ever-increasing insistence as I yield all open yes to the licks of the fire quivering in anticipation of the inexorable penetration of a sword yet receiving this slow dark thrust of primordial tenderness brooding over a rising flood that catches me sighing my surrender

haloed moon . . .
a storm gathers
in darkness

I am a sea of dark waves rising and heaving in an intensifying swell with all my darkness moving as my depths part and roll asunder to you plunging deeper and deeper uncovering the depths of me thrusting yes closer and closer yes touching closer into yes the unknown and further the waves roll apart until yes with a soft shuddering convulsion I know myself found

before dawn
the mystery
is complete

♡

*summer night
kissed by the moon . . .
isis temple*

awake, these hot
summer nights my body
glowing . . .
fires of passion
erupt in my heart

an apple
bitten to the core . . .
summer paradise

two clouds
in a blue sky . . .
merging

the moon
ripples into shore . . .
sipping
forever dreams
of your nakedness

a dream
I once had . . .
sleep

asleep . . .
your heartbeat
in my ear

44

:-)
:-(

taking turns
to egg each other on —
nahaiwrimo

plum blossoms
in the paris metro . . .
pounded faces

frog spawn
in a muddy ditch —
sound of splooge

dry weather —
the poodle waters
what it can

without plum blossom . . .
the frogpond's smound

river's edge . . .
a haijin jumps into
the sound of snoring

a red ant . . .
not impressed
by my foot

rain puddle . . .
my image shivers
in silence

morning dew . . .
I search the web
for moth husks

wolf moon . . .
what big eyes
you have

spring shower . . .
in the fountain
more rings

bathroom spider —
finding only wet tales
in its web

tell me wolf,
does size really
matter?

the words
she never believed —
paper moon

a matter of faith
once in a blue moon

lost trail —
smoke rises
from a tipi

distant signals
of a nomadic tribe —
spring hopes

sound of wings flapping
a condor lands in the tree

from the brink
a bird of distinction —
promises made

dawn
looming from the shadows
a tree

first light . . .
out of the shadows
a deer

early light —
the red deer hind
rubs a tree

morning glow . . .
from the darkness again,
a tui's call

blackbird season —
the pupil nurses
a smacked hand

in this light
the aha of critics —
blackbirds flying

winter rain . . .
moving under the lilac
a blackbird's eye

winter sky —
a crow answers
my cold call

without
a single word . . .
summer

spring shower
her hairdryer sizzles
to life

winter solstice . . .
car headlights stretch out
across the night

winter ocean —
your peace within a ring
of fire

muddy pond . . .
another prince charming
disappears

shrouded hills —
the cry of the poor
in my ears

spring dawn —
railroad tracks merging
on the horizon

tidal moon —
where does the sun rise
tomorrow?

cyber moon —
our heartbeats
refresh

boxing day —
fresh cardboard boxes
for the homeless

gutted tv—
where lies your reality
now?

launching a droid
into the galaxy . . .
spring of words

miss august
curls at the edges . . .
end of summer

satellite dish
looming over a shack . . .
winter moon

recycling bin —
she checks out online
dating

kicking stars —
old men still boys
with jelly knees

high wind —
the farmer harvests
amps

long distance
shorter than my dime . . .
shooting star

bitter spring—
not all ducks
are paired

haiku pond . . .
the ripples left
behind

aha—
such an anticlimax
the cherry on top

summer plenty—
how the other half
lives

dry pond . . .
the serenade of a frog
in the night

mother tongue—
all of the books
left behind

in the pond
one drip, one ring . . .
now I lose count

sunset moon—
the tales they make
us believe

The Dark Night

I see the best minds of my generation lacking all conviction, circling the carrion of their own reflection like indignant desert birds. To ipod-driven sounds their loins shudder into each other with mechanical desperation drowning out the terror pounding in their hearts.

blackbird,
what visions sustain
your song?

invisible clouds
darken the night sky . . .
glowing hands
on my father's watch
show almost midnight

wet eyes
peer over a white mask . . .
the shadows
of mushroom clouds,
shrouding the sun

a novice poet
emerges from her secret room
to summer's last light . . .
in an act of reverence
she gifts the earth her stool

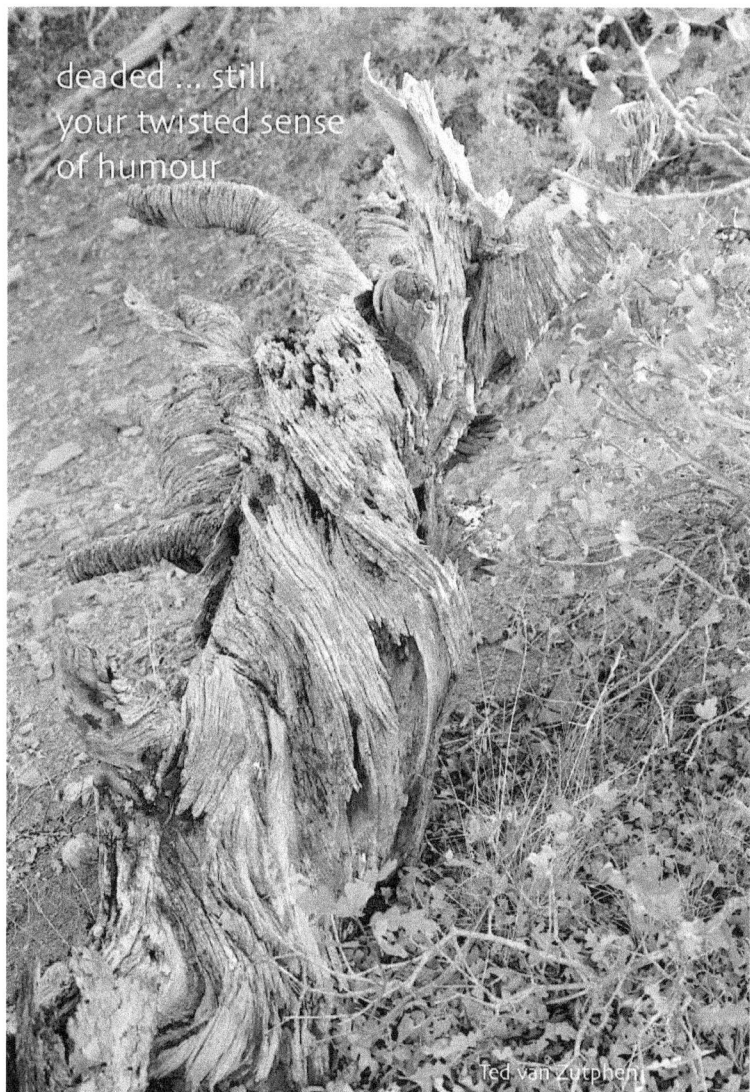

deaded ... still
your twisted sense
of humour

Ted van Zutphen

year's end—
no more leaves
to turn

summer quake —
here, a snowdrop
tolls

Svetlana

*swan song . . .
the limb-loosening rush
of dark feathers*

Death and the Maiden

In this desolate valley, a sound ... rasping ... the sound of a rusty gate on rusted hinges moved by wind. The air is still.

Following after the sound I find the source barely distinguishable from the dry dust of the desert. Movement ... a rising and falling ... rasping. A form ... desiccated ... possibly human ... rasping ... drained of all moisture ... rasping ... and finally with a sigh ... a breath of wind.

I become aware of a sneering laugh moving into the valley from the encircling desert ... a laugh of mockery and victory that just as suddenly transforms into a howl of utter horror, loss and desolation. This sound fades away ... with whimpering ...into the distant cities.

I turn my eyes to the dried out body of the unfortunate creature as a green shoot uncurls slowly from the split open chest.

desert thirst . . .
the hyena's victory
in a howl

desert thirst ...
the hyena's victory
in a howl

silent vigil . . .
a monk pierces the clouds
with closed eyes

a heavy sky
deepening the silence
within

autumn mist
first grey then gold . . .
morning fire

name day . . .
the smoothness of
a white stone

lenten journey
each pilgrim prepares
their own cilice

passion fruit
journeying to dust . . .
ash wednesday

lenten journey . . .
before the canoeist's axe
a fallen tree

blisters
from a moccasin
not mine

lenten reflection . . .
a wanderer explores
her journal

singing alone
the child chains daisies . . .
autumn dusk

silent reflection . . .
for an instant I know
in being known

from the mists
something drifts into view . . .
swan song

Out of the Cloister

As young as she feels and as old as her habit, she takes pen to paper struggling against the worm that secretly nibbles away her life. All that fills her mind she caresses, as if for the first time ... the cry of a morepork, the howls of King Lear, the ecstasy of San Juan de la Cruz, the scent of a rose.

baring more
than her heart—
full moon

stillness . . .
after the rainbow
fades

winter lake
reflecting cloudy days
without a ripple

ponga fronds
laid out under the moon —
a path less travelled

lenten journey . . .
all that I cling to
is shaken away

frigid air . . .
the emptiness
left by your words

bitter spring . . .
the root bound
cherry tree

autumn rain —
a leaf falls within
loneliness

autumn rain —
the sound of leaf fall
drowning

autumn rain —
entering the grayness
only dusk

autumn rain —
the colour of birdsong
smudging

falling leaf,
do you forget
your roots?

overnight rain—
even our differences
wash away

a distant train
pierces the darkness . . .
lenten silence

last supper—
the covenant of love
in this cup

Good Friday —
the transformation
still to come

stillness —
the decay of the apple
on the tree

empty cross —
the splinters of love
in the dirt

Let There Be

yes I do not know who I am sleeping and my
breathing in and out with sand flowing from my
fingers and toes into the air like the incense I like the
smell of after benediction and the footsteps that take
me into the ocean that absorbs all sound when my feet
find the wet sand sinking through my toes with the
pull of the sea not cold but the coolness of this
vastness rippling around my thighs lapping against
my maidenhead and goosebumps expecting what
revelation will come with this breath sounds
somewhere in and around me oh yes

Lord Jesus Christ, son of God, have mercy on me, a sinner.

after dark —
the glossolalia
of the sea

 yes I am the Samaritan lady at the well with the
middle eastern sun and sand the man asks me to draw
water for him his eyes not undressing me like men do
since I began to shape into a woman but he yes he sees
me and asks me yes for water yet he asks me to see
who he is that I if I ask he will give me living water
and I am not just a sinner but a creature in a desert
thirsting and this man is offering me water that will

never stop like a spring welling up like this
quickening that loosens in me yes

Lord Jesus Christ, son of God, have mercy on me, a sinner.

autumn night
unfolding before my eyes
from nothing

 but God is silent existing only in an unapproachable
light on the other side of all that is outside of the
vastness of space and the billion upon billions of years
of time when change first began the way my heart
burns within me and the quickening I feel like it must
feel to have a baby growing inside my womb if I put
frangipani flowers in my hair or jasmine like the other
girls and wear a pretty yes and welcome his kiss in a
shady grove and I am wanting him more than any
other and then I ask him with my eyes to find me and
yes he would seek and yes I would

Lord Jesus Christ, son of God, have mercy on me, a sinner.

frogpond —
the forgotten silence
of tadpoles

closer to me than I am myself filling my innermost self
knowing my weaknesses and aches in ways that are
too big for me to grasp for when I think I know it flits
by yes he is in all I know from the light of stars long
long gone to the edge of swelling space from the seed
of my birth to the void of my death in every fold of my
body every beat of my heart every stirring of my mind
and yes again parting the petals of my lips and yes my
light my arms around and yes drawing him down to
my breasts all yielding yes

Lord Jesus Christ, son of God, have mercy on me, a sinner.

in the wind
what might have been . . .
sleepless moon

 yes the emptiness not even lightning can illuminate
parts for me and I hear breathing as of some long
forgotten coupling while a dark wind broods with
warm breast and with yes bright wings

first light . . .
for a moment all colour
is this

the precision
with which my shadow
anticipates
my every move
as I make my move

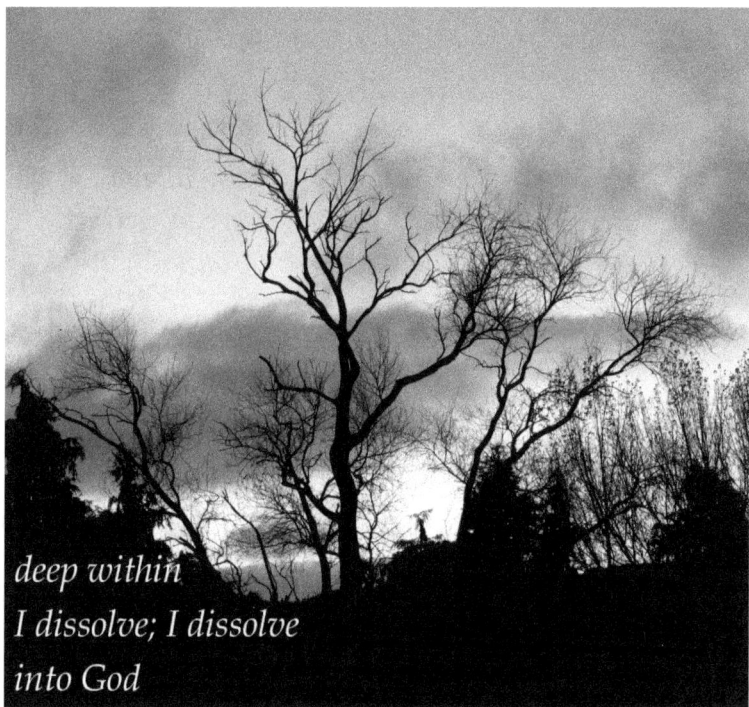

deep within
I dissolve; I dissolve
into God

filled
to overflowing . . .
crescent moon

coming dawn . . .
river fog curls
around light

river stars . . .
total immersion
in the night

garden gate . . .
that tree stays just
out of reach

moon flower —
glimpses of more
within grasp

so simple
the way dewdrops
leave

first words . . .
bringing to light
your voice

apple core . . .
losing the stairway
to heaven

prayer time . . .
snow flakes melting
on my palms

ancient wind . . .
a brooding dove
descends

moonless night —
the emptiness
being filled

last light . . .
again I surrender
to the unknown

ancient stars
what light will be shed
tonight?

distant thunder . . .
the invisible worm
laying in wait

stretched
to its limit—
spring

the space
being emptied of nothing . . .
full moon

Mt Taranaki . . .
maintaining the dormancy
I cannot

twilight —
the chrysalis
forming

The Golden Calf

At a specific moment when light has not yet formed, when birds tune up for the sun rise, between the lightning and the thunder, the questing minds of men and women, too numerous to number with any accuracy, gathered to give voice to the mysteries that haunted every waking and sleeping moment since humankind, with their backs to the darkness, began to name what they could see.

One spoke: "From the beginning of recorded time our kind has given words to all things that we see, hear, taste, touch and smell. We have even formed words together to describe things that we can only imagine made from what we have already named and, in time, form new things. Yet still each of us has a lonely sadness that lingers like the morning mists on a sunless day. What we have not done is to face the encircling darkness naked without recourse to what we have named. Maybe it is only that way that we can discover the contentment that eternally eludes each of us."

Individuals from each of all the known philosophies, mythologies, religions, arts and sciences, both recorded and those long forgotten in time, spoke. Each discipline had its opportunity to present what it had to offer - among them ontologists, cosmologists, mathematicians, physicians, chemists, biologists, philosophers, Moslems, Shamans, Christians, Jews, Buddhists, Hindus, animists, paleontologists, explorers, soldiers, engineers, painters, sculptors, painters, novelists and poets.

Every speaker was listened to with hushed respect as each presentation gave another surface to the jewel that was forming from the human journey.

Once all that needed to be said was said all viewed the wondrous embodiment. There was no question that the object was of the greatest beauty ever formed by humanity, forming and reforming, creating and destroying, singing and wailing, uplifting and casting down, filled with agony and ecstasy. All admired it without reserve bursting with joy overwhelmed that the whole universe suddenly made sense.

This moment soon passed and the ache moved once more through the assembly as slowly each participant began to leave tossing a glance of desperate sadness at the idol they had crafted.

As they left a young girl rushed with eager step offering her baby for each she met to hold for a moment.

the universe
suddenly personal . . .
newborn child

midnight heat . . .
darkness pregnant
with a girl

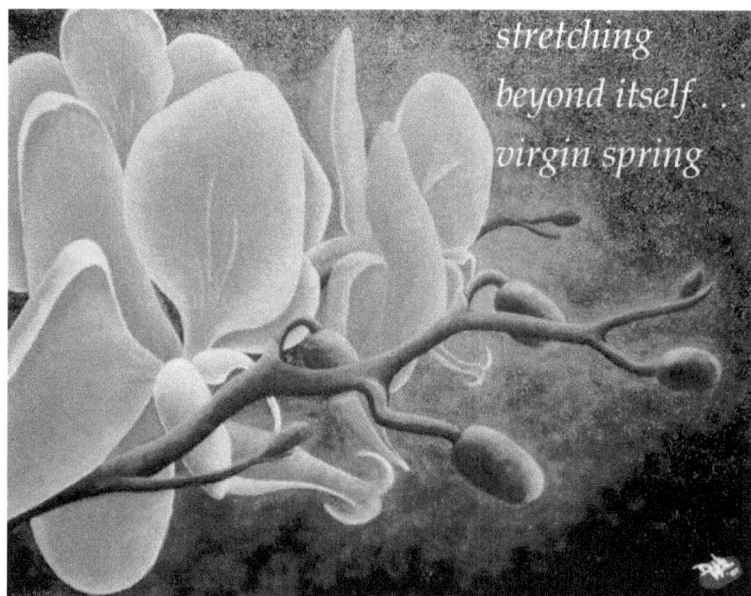

stretching
beyond itself . . .
virgin spring

distant chant . . .
moonlight seeping
through incense

open fire . . .
my haiku curls
inwards

freshening breeze . . .
butterflies crinkle
the surface

blackbird,
each day your song
summons dawn

this haiku —
all that I leave out
still present

a sparrow
rides a Japanese maple . . .
winter wind

silent bird,
I carry your song
through shadows

the distance
between dusk and dawn —
deep waters

all the stars
no longer seen —
sleepless night

the lonely
yoking of words
through the night

unsung song
being composed
breath by breath

the journey
of a lifetime —
this dark night

waning moon
also awake
beyond dawn

day by day
baptismal rain . . .
open hands

sister rain,
can we wash this world
clean?

Jesus beads
anchoring me
to each breath

winter orchestra . . .
the necessity
of a blackbird

this descant
in winter shadows . . .
silent prayer

transforming
within her hand . . .
hailstone beads

winter evening
present in its approach . . .
a sitting blackbird

winter darkness . . .
harvesting the light
of dead stars

winter chill . . .
the last shadows of dawn
or blackbirds

icy wind —
the bare branch scratches
an epitaph

The Lady

The parchment touch of her hand flutters weakly within the supple warmth of mine as I read quietly to her from Doctor Zhivago. Other words do not seem to have a place as stillness settles within a summer evening's light.

ravages of winter
on the grave's mound
as her presence fades

I leave behind
the light of bridges
still burning

river fog
moving over the fields . . .
blackbird in flight

icy moon
all over the valley
unveiling . . .

bathing
in your reflected glory —
full moon

full moon —
I too reflect
on the day

fading light . . .
my eyes follow
a mayfly

here comes
everyone — a lone
a last a loved

distant sun . . .
dewdrops clinging
to branches

lenten silence . . .
a dew drop trickles
to the ground

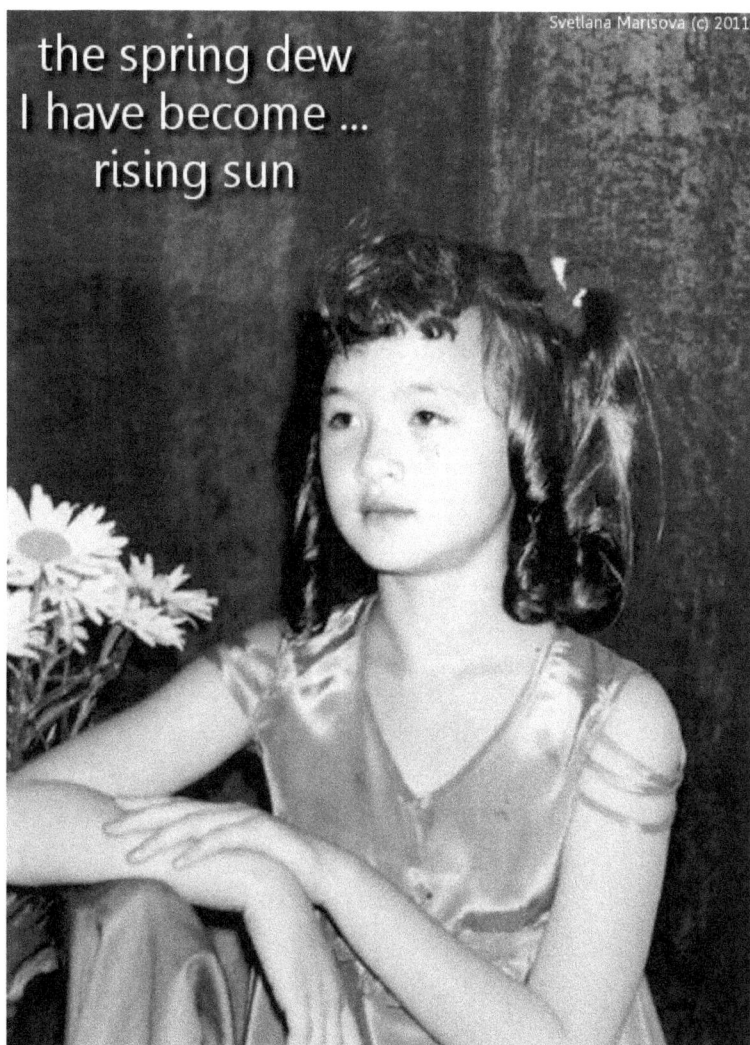

the spring dew
I have become ...
rising sun

Svetlana Marisova (c) 2011

Ted

the warmth
of comfortable silence . . .
winter dusk

this stone
in my pocket . . .
memories
that become lighter
with every step

a bee's dance
from bloom to bloom . . .
end of spring

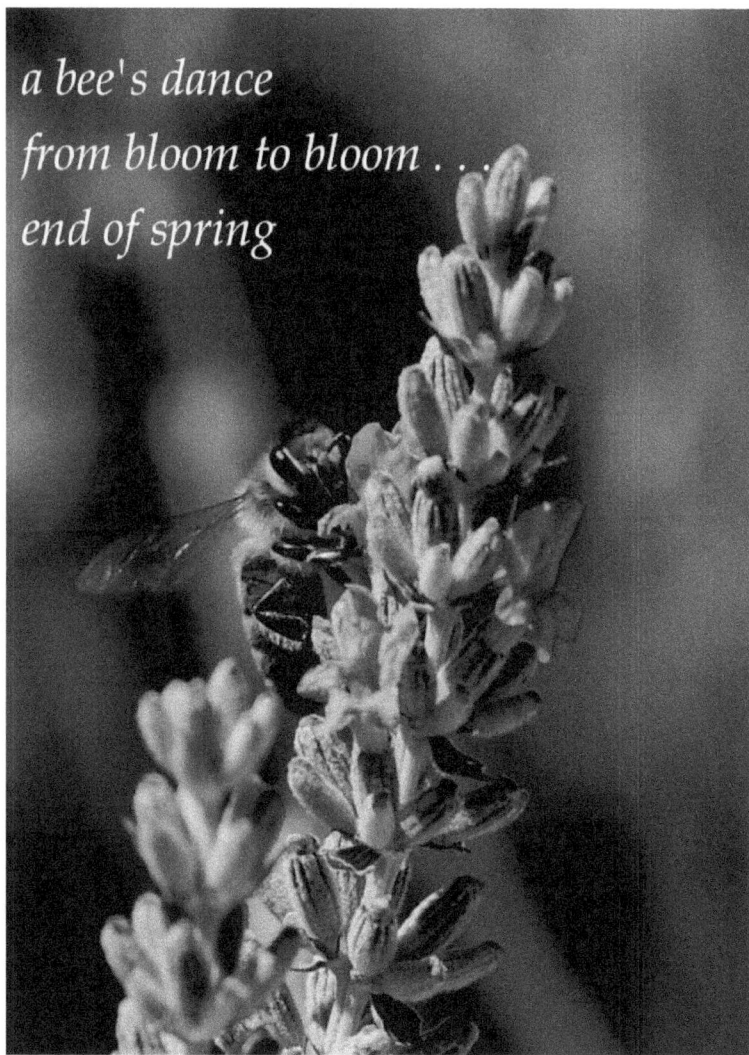

fresh snow
yesterday's tracks
gone

the glacier
calving an iceberg —
another candle

winter silence —
a squirrel scampers,
stops . . . and prays

winter thaw —
the chipmunk eyes
snowman's eyes

turning over
another leaf—
paper cut

hyacinth—
spring fever floods
my frozen nose

cat song
resonating in a dream . . .
summer moon

hunger moon . . .
an acorn shimmers
through melting snow

his dog,
with every sound, her ears
. . . sunset's green flash

aftershock—
last heartbeat
in the street

snow-white lily
the drum skin's
tremble

summer's end—
the blind dog spots
doll's eyes

leaves of fall
still decomposing . . .
sacred spring

sunrise . . .
clouds chase the shadow
of a tree

washed out notes
in my jean jacket —
spring cleaning

early spring . . .
feeding my hungry nose
a hyacinth

new rising sun —
when is late
too late?

smoke rings
roll around my finger . . .
train whistle

sunrise
warming my heart . . .
autumn chill

running with horses . . . endless spring

A new journey begins with the wrenching away from the old familiar. Change has come from a direction I am unprepared for. Maisie, my baby, now old, deaf, mostly blind and feeble, still relishes to be by my side. When awake, her eyes follow my shadow if her legs can't and she begs me to be near her.

In the weeks leading up to our planned departure, she has become weaker and weaker, becoming less able to sustain her body with food and drink. Some days she seems to almost wither away and I pray for her to stay in her sleep peacefully, but then she magically revives the next day with a willful sense of loyalty. At long last even her devotion to me is no longer enough. She asks me to let her go and travel alone.

last breath —
a raindrop sizzles
on glowing embers

I wrap her up in her pooh bear blanket and the next morning we bury her 16 year old lifeless body next to Erving, her father, in the back yard. Certainly the best place for her final resting place, with all the family pets of the last 25 years: our cats Eleanor, Butch, Ursula and Frankie, our dogs Thea, Critter and Erving and three still born puppies, several rats, hamsters, an iguana, water dragon, many goldfish and more than 80 budgies and finches.

dust settles
in my garden . . .
sleeping moon

As I set out on my journey, I know she's still with me,
watching and protecting me, sitting in the passenger seat or
on my lap. Man or dog better not come close to us, or she'll
protect me with her life. She so loves traveling, getting her
head in the wind, looking out the window, taking
everything in and not passing a chance to bark at other dogs
as we drive by. Her favorite spot is on my shoulders and
neck, where she can have a good view of everything. "Dogs
Love Trucks" is her.

midnight train—
whistling the dream,
that was

We stop at a meadow, where some horses graze and
leisurely come and check us out. Her kinship with them is
uncanny. Other large animals, dogs, cows and man, she
shows no respect and attacks without fear, but horses are
another story. She just stares at them in awe. I am sure, she
has been one in a previous incarnation or wants to be one
when she grows up…

at the door
still her leash . . .
moonshadow

sickle moon . . .
from behind clouds
your reflection,
a faint glimmer stills
waves on the dark horizon

fading stars . . .
still your warmth
with me

unleashed . . .
she carries me
on her wings

misty morning—
the dogwood blooms
my breath

this snail
taking his shell . . .
where?

riverbank . . .
willow branches reach
for their roots

shrouded mountains . . .
your presence pierces
the distance

oh rock . . .
how long will it take
to wear you down?

even the river,
flowing to its destiny . . .
remains of the day

high noon —
a cloud evaporates
. . . reforms

waves speaking
in ancient tongues . . .
spring morning

fresh leaves
feed the iris . . .
sipping haiku

super moon
the tide returns . . .
yesterday

morning dew . . .
words unspoken
fill the void

the words
that never end . . .
slow river

an ant
carries more than its weight
morning prayer

sunday morning
in the shadow of our church
my climbing tree

hiding moon —
still the bloodstains
on his hands

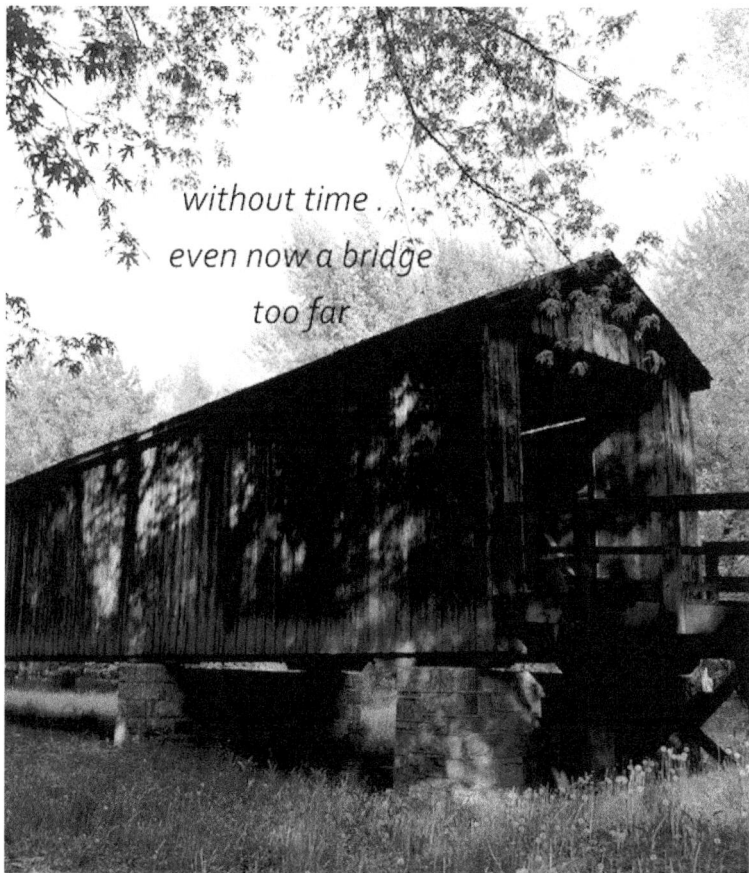

without time . . .
even now a bridge
too far

Be Still and Know . . .

crashing waves —
almost believing
it's forever

roaring river . . .
one pebble at a time,
carving temples

pearl diving . . .
haiku and tumours
from the depths

blood sucker -
this life being probed
is mine

drowning sun —
my fingers hover
not finding words

shortening days . . .
the time left to complete
my epitaph

egg moon —
the time between hope
and memories

lengthening nights
the distance between
each ebb and flow

river tide . . .
where do we go
from here?

remission . . .
learning to bear the beams
of love

autumn burial . . .
the ripening of seed sown
in darkness

remembering
my flawless memory . . .
red river

red cloud
in the garden
wormwood

holy ground —
before the door
a doormat

distant stars —
doors of perception
opening

through
the front door —
night

setting moon . . .
the wall between us
brick by brick

now open
without a key . . .
doors of perception

Joan of Arc —
words of love forming
from the smoke

my image
two inches behind
your eyes

the butterfly . . .
its tingle as it leaves
my hand

autumn dusk . . .
an angel of light
casts a shadow

winter night —
I let his longing
warm mine

foggy moon . . .
where can I pay back
borrowed time?

fantail,
when you stop flitting,
so will I

river breeze —
the bamboo again
rustles your name

winter chill . . .
the whitespace between
these lines

mourning dove —
the time it takes to catch
a glimpse of you

first light . . .
today on the edge
of eternity

floating downstream —
the burden of my shadow
on a mayfly

Naming Trees

Slipping away unnoticed from the billowing mists of the ever restless throng, I enter my secret room. Breathing deeply my lungs fill to capacity then slowly exhale until I can breathe out no more. Repeating this several times sounds outside the room merge with sounds inside the room losing distinction and meaning as I become detached even from the sound of my own breathing and the slow steady beat of my heart.

prayer time —
a breath of wind
passes by

Radiance of morning, pukekos high-stepping through incandescent dew, blackbirds rejoicing in it while the urgency of a fantail leads me towards something sweeter than love. The sun, the warmth, the play of light bouncing off the river's flow, off leaves of grass and trees in countless variations of green, the sound of insects humming through tall grasses and shrubs, the song and flutter of flitting birds, the sublime vacancy of sky, paddock, bush and my own heart.

silent bird,
I carry your song
through shadows

Alone along I venture through light-dappled forest tracks
to God knows what revelation reciting the litany of sacred
names as I pass them - horopito, towai, kamahi, puriri,
mapou, horoeka, totara, matai, miro, rimu, kahikatea, karo,
tarata, tanekaha.

tree of life—
your branches summon
this fallen child;
knowing in being so known
your mystery enfolds me

Suddenly personal

the softness
of baby skin . . .
ladyhawke

*As I sit in the hospital room, I look down upon this
precious bundle in my lap, my new grand daughter, so
peacefully sleeping into this new life and so totally present
in every moment. But contained in this miracle I feel the
hopes and dreams of my daughter and her husband, the
heartaches and the happiness, the worries and the
fulfillment, the battles and the victories, the nightmares and
the comfort, the pride, the mystery, the love... yes, always
the love, unconditional love.*

ancient trail
into the canyon . . .
new moon

*I think of the mother, who, many moons ago, cradled her
newborn daughter and held those same hopes and dreams
for her, now struggling and facing the biggest challenge this
life offers us. Hope turned into hopelessness, dreams turned
into nightmares, smiles turned to tears, but still the love…
boundless love.*

summer rain—
only half of me . . .
rippled

Later I step into the darkness from my daughter's house and walk along the path to my mobile home. I lift my head to the heavens… a haloed moon stares back at me and I hear the surges of crickets shifting from tree to tree. My breath continues… "Be still, and know that I am God"

newborn star . . .
dried up tears falling
in my lap

full moon
on a bed of clouds . . .
the smile
I can't forget
out-shining stars

I too
am earthbound . . .
lingering moon

tree of life—
revealing her perfection
inside the womb

the big bang's
ejaculation of stars—
moonless night

waxing moon . . .
the longing that
cycles back

a garter snake
leaves his skin behind . . .
spring dawn

stillness . . .
the coolness of air
on my skin

rustling leaves . . .
the infinite silence
in these words

morning mist—
even this sound
must die

spider silk
enmeshing the dawn -
a world of dew

resting leaf—
this was her garden seat
last year

morning moon —
even the hummingbird
takes a breather

autumn dusk . . .
she swings through light
while it lasts

moon child . . .
the flower in her hair,
wilted

hell's angel —
a downs syndrome girl
takes his hand

a beetle
burrows into the tree . . .
impending cyclone

fading storm —
a beetle crawls out
to see the light

autistic child —
the coffin she christens
a boat

distant echoes . . .
I learn the lines
of loss

final act —
facing the death scene
without a script

broken mirror —
he steps on a high wire
without safety net

the choices
not so clear now . . .
twilight

sapling oak —
still in the shadow
of a dying willow

sinking sun . . .
the seagull pecks
a wormhole

myriad birds . . .
the dawn chorus
on stage

paper crane —
silence enfolds
my breath

solar flare . . .
catching alight
far too soon

bitter fruit . . .
tasting only
not being

candle wax
suffocates the flame . . .
morning star

untapped spring . . .
caressing the hardness
of the rock

winter frenzy . . .
raindrops wearing down
river stones

horizon
of grief . . . too fast
this meteor

sister rain,
the fullness of your love
overwhelms me

morning prayer . . .
the will, I have to live
without

lullabies —
your peaceful sleep
enfolding

winter sun . . .
another flash
in the pan

Rosary

At the mention of his name the light in her eyes turns in while stillness overwhelms the fumbling crawl of her fingers over the beads.

sizzling tears . . .
even these embers
unquenched

kuaka —
our migrant hearts skirting
the ring of fire

autumn twilight . . .
I linger between daydreams
and nightmares

feijoa —
you also decay
too soon

silent river —
the crickets also
do not hear it

the winter stealth
of a daddy longlegs
in my eyes . . .

blossom shower . . .
even our differences
beautiful

the weight
of being different . . .
black swan

stepping back
into my footprints —
summer dreams

morphine . . .
again my dreams
submerging

winter surf . . .
the constant heartbeat
of my dreams

night crawler . . .
the pain of dreams
rupturing

my dreams
still chasing svetulya . . .
haloed moon

algal bloom
enters my dreams . . .
brimming words

fading moon . . .
the dreams that came
and went

from my dreams
distant rumbling . . .
spider web

night breeze . . .
ashes peel off
dying embers

cold morning . . .
reality drifts back
as a dream

slipping through
my negligée —
morning mist

midnight prayer . . .
a mayfly floats
into the moon

the light
of yesterday's hope . . .
sunrise

winter shadows
rooted to the earth . . .
windy night

leaves curling
on a peach tree . . .
bitter fruit

winter gloom . . .
an ecstatic thrush
sings on

this pain
behind the eyes —
gloomy night

moonless night . . .
my name sinking
into stone

bruised feijoa,
the rot begins
within

the smile
of his approach . . .
waxing moon

oh tui . . .
I'm anxious to hear
your next song

twilight star . . .
a tui breaks the day
here too

waning moon —
a rosebud trembles,
waits its turn . . .

flickering star . . .
can you see the new moon
from there?

still mountain . . .
your words passing
through me

mountain fog . . .
feeling a cloud slip
through my fingers

burying
my placenta,
between stars

seeing
the unseen
in fog

rising mist . . .
a godwit tears away
from its reflection

a doe . . .
drinking from the light
of dawn

between
the words you breathe . . .
divine light

wind-borne waif . . .
the life I caress
with each breath

within
your every breath . . .
one word

summer's end . . .
light pirouettes
one last time

a mayfly
borrowing time . . .
last dance

teach me, candle,
the art of becoming —
as fire

the tree,
without leaves, still
breathing . . .

unnoticed,
the godwit's tear
flowing south

oh tree,
how will we survive
this winter?

black swans
ravishing light
just like that

morepork,
what colour is
a last breath?

dormant moon . . .
your epiphany
awaits me

tui,
I too delight
in this world

closed daisies . . .
the chain a child
makes of stars

autumn rain . . .
the mirror in a night
of tears

half moon . . .
the other half
lingers

end of summer —
between a crow's caws
church bells ring

scenting
the angelus bell . . .
wild roses

solitude . . .
embracing a star
in the desert

shrouded night . . .
I etch my will
into stone

lost moon . . .
the coldness of
that tear

twilight breeze . . .
a dark night stirs
in the earth

autumn arbour . . .
a grasshopper snaps
its wings

the eyes,
that keep feeding me
the same word . . .
how can the sun not
rise again tomorrow?

flashlit eyes –
the dream of being
someone's dream

silent night . . .
the flute hiding
in bamboo

twilight wind . . .
coolness rippling
on my skin

harvest moon,
dream into me
through the night . . .

our last touch
through the looking-glass . . .
moonlight shadow

misty dawn . . .
how i hunger for you
to lift that veil
and reveal today's beauty
all over again

godwit's flight . . .
light disappearing
with the sun

Cape Reinga . . .
merging between the waves
early mist

rising mist . . .
the poem ends
'with thanks'

forgotten moon —
carved in the night sky,
my deathday

entwined
memories embrace
the future past

oneness now . . .
the caress of your lips
tasting my words

please tui,
can you wake me again
before dawn?

yes —
Penelope's
last word

.

www.ingramcontent.com/pod-product-compliance
Lightning Source LLC
LaVergne TN
LVHW051404080426
835508LV00022B/2973